Jim Kelly

by Mark Stewart

ACKNOWLEDGMENTS
The editors wish to thank Jim Kelly for his cooperation in preparing this book.
Thanks also to Integrated Sports International for their assistance.

PHOTO CREDITS
All photos courtesy AP/Wide World Photos, Inc. except the following:

Vince Manniello/Sports Chrome – cover
Rob Tringali Jr./Sports Chrome – 5 top
Jim Kelly – 4 top left, 8, 9, 10, 13, 24, bottom left 43 top

STAFF
Project Coordinator: John Sammis, Cronopio Publishing
Series Design Concept: The Sloan Group
Design and Electronic Page Makeup: Jaffe Enterprises, and
        Digital Communications Services, Inc.

LIBRARY OF CONGRESS CATALOGING-IN-PUBLICATION DATA
Stewart, Mark.
    Jim Kelly / by Mark Stewart.
        p. cm. – (Grolier all-pro biographies)
    Includes index.
    Summary: Covers the personal life and football career of the star quarterback for the Buffalo
Bills.
        ISBN 0-516-20143-3 (lib. binding)–ISBN 0-516-26007-3 (pbk.)
    1. Kelly, Jim, 1960-   –Juvenile literature. 2. Football players–United States–
Biography–Juvenile literature. 3. Buffalo Bills (Football team)–Juvenile literature.
(1. Kelly, Jim, 1960- . 2. Football players.)
I. Title. II. Series.
GV939.K37S84 1996
796.332'092–dc20
(B)   96-33789
                                                                                               CIP
                                                                                               AC

Grolier ALL-PRO Biographies™

Jim Kelly

by
Mark Stewart

CHILDREN'S PRESS®
A Division of Grolier Publishing
New York • London • Hong Kong • Sydney
Danbury, Connecticut

Contents

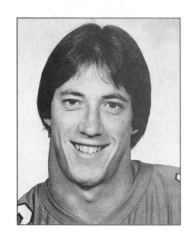

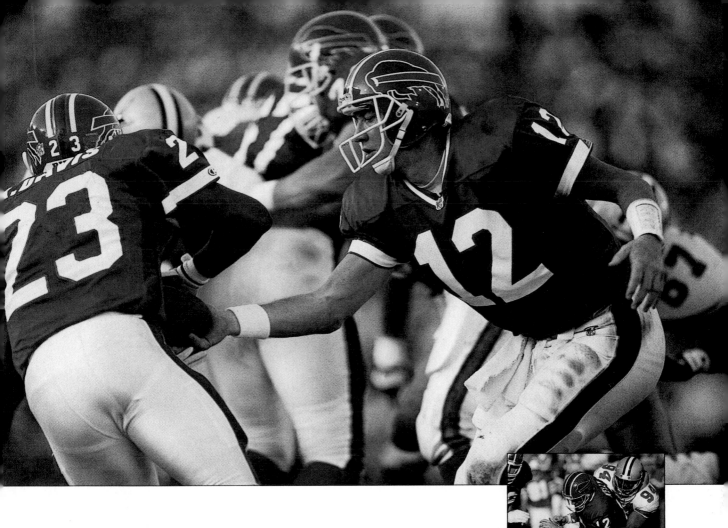

Who

Am I?

hen you are one of six brothers, you learn how to survive. You learn how to give a solid hit and you learn how to take one. You also learn that sometimes, no matter what you do, you're going to end up on the bottom of a big pile! I guess all that banging around I did as a kid prepared me for life as an NFL quarterback. I don't really enjoy getting knocked on my rear by a 350-pound pass rusher, but I don't mind it all that much either. Some say I'm tough. Others say I'm just a big kid. The truth is that I'm a little of both. My name is Jim Kelly, and this is my story . . ."

"You learn how to survive."

Growing Up

I f anyone was born to be a quarterback, it would have to be Jim Kelly. He was just a toddler when he first picked up a football, but Jim threw a perfect spiral to his father. By the age of six, Jim was holding his own in the tackle football games he and his brothers played in the living room. And when he turned eight, Jim joined a Midget Football team and became its star end. By this time, Jim's dad knew his son was something special. He encouraged Jim to practice his throwing and kicking. Joe Kelly even met his son during lunch breaks to help him practice.

Growing up in East Brady, Pennsylvania, Jim had two favorite players. One was Joe Namath of the New York Jets, who had grown up in the nearby town of Beaver Falls. The other was Terry Bradshaw of the Steelers, who played in

Jim Kelly, age six months

At East Brady High, Jim starred in football and basketball.

Pittsburgh, just a couple of hours away. At the age of 10, Jim signed up for the Punt, Pass, and Kick contest, and he advanced to the regional semifinals. The competition was held during half-time of a Steelers game. Jim was excited to win the event in front of thousands of people. But the biggest thrill was meeting his idol, Terry Bradshaw. At that point, Jim was so sure he would be a pro quarterback that he actually practiced signing his own autograph!

Jim's father, Joe, worked in a factory. His mother, Alice, worked in a school cafeteria when she was not taking care of

Jim (with ball), with his mother and brothers Kevin and Dan

her six boys. The Kellys did not have a lot of money, and everyone had to help out. To earn a few dollars for himself, Jim shoveled snow in the winter and mowed lawns in the summer. Sometimes, when money was very tight, Jim and his brothers had to chip in some of their own money so the family could afford groceries.

Jim loved growing up in East Brady, a friendly, small town with a population of about eight hundred. His family lived so close to school that he could see it from his house. Jim remembers, "East Brady had no stop lights, no fast food restaurants, no anything. It seemed like almost everybody in my town was athletically inclined, and we all wanted to be the best at whatever we did, whether it was whiffle ball, stickball, or throwing rocks out into the Allegheny River. We were always competing against one another. And that's probably why I am where I am today."

When Jim was 11, he learned a hard lesson about being a team player. Because he was so much bigger than the other children his age, he had to be weighed before each youth league game to make sure he did not exceed the 132-pound limit. The night before the championship game, he ate a huge meal of hot dogs, soda, and other junk food. The next morning, Jim weighed in at 133 pounds and was not allowed to play. His team lost the game, and Jim felt horrible. In fact, he still considers it the worst moment of his football career.

His favorite subject was math, and he liked English, too. He got As and Bs in almost all of his classes. Jim had some trouble with social studies, but he concentrated harder on those assignments and read very carefully to make sure he understood everything. Today, Jim still recognizes the value of good reading skills. "I can't see how a person can go through life not knowing how to read well—whether it's a newspaper, a sign, or instructions on medicine. You cannot get through a day in this society without knowing how to read."

Jim's favorite teacher was a man named George Geiser. He was very demanding and made Jim work as hard as he could. He also looked up to him because he knew Mr. Geiser was a superb athlete. Mr. Geiser helped to teach Jim that he should never allow sports to interfere with his schoolwork. That same lesson was taught at home by Jim's father. Joe Kelly told all of his boys that a big part of being a great athlete was being able to think quickly. And the only way to train your mind is to excel in school. Jim took this advice seriously, and he discovered that competing in the classroom could be just as exciting as competing in sports. As it turned out, Jim's father was right. When the college recruiters began scouting Jim, they all agreed that he possessed a special combination of toughness and intelligence.

Jim continued to grow quickly. Throughout high school, he was always bigger, better, stronger, and faster than other boys his age. He became the starting quarterback for East Brady High School when he was 16. But Jim's impact went beyond signal-calling on offense. When East Brady went on defense, Jim stayed on the field as the team's top tackler! In his junior and senior years, Jim led East Brady to two straight undefeated seasons and league championships. If that wasn't enough, Jim also excelled at basketball. He averaged 23 points and 20 rebounds a game during his senior year.

Jim's father and mother look on as he signs papers for the University of Miami.

Jim had long dreamed of playing football at Penn State University. The school had a glorious football history, and Jim admired Penn State's football coach, Joe Paterno. So Jim was thrilled when Coach Paterno watched him play. Paterno offered Jim a scholarship to attend Penn State and play defense. He said that Jim could likely become an All-America linebacker. That was good news and bad news for Jim. He felt honored to be recruited by Paterno, but he was disappointed that Paterno did not believe Jim could make it at quarterback. Heartbroken, Jim turned down Penn State and decided to attend the University of Miami.

College

For most of Jim's first year in college, he wondered if he had made a terrible mistake in choosing the University of Miami. He enjoyed his classes and loved Florida's warm winters, but what he saw on the football field scared him to death. From what Jim could see, coach Lou Saban did nothing but scream at his quarterbacks, call them names, and make fun of them. Even though Jim was red-shirted (ineligible to play) his freshman year, he thought how miserable it would be when Coach Saban began yelling at him the following fall.

Jim was relieved when the school hired a new coach named Howard Schnellenberger, who

Earl Morrall (right) taught Jim many of the secrets of playing quarterback.

Years

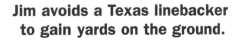

Jim avoids a Texas linebacker to gain yards on the ground.

seemed to be in Jim's corner from the start. He also began working with Earl Morrall, a former NFL star. Morrall taught Jim how to read defenses and change the speed of his throws to suit specific situations. Jim improved rapidly, but he still did not think he would play much in his first active season. Although he was as talented as the team's starting quarterback, he lacked the experience to run the team. Or so he thought.

Coach Schnellenberger had other ideas. The day of Miami's big game against Penn State, Jim was eating his pre-game meal. He was thinking that it would be satisfying to defeat the same team that had said he was not good enough to be a quarterback. Just then, Coach Schnellenberger called him over and told him he would be the starting quarterback! The coach knew how badly Jim wanted to be a winner, and beating Joe Paterno's

Nittany Lions would be a once-in-a-lifetime opportunity to show what he had.

In front of 70,000 stunned fans, Jim—a complete unknown—cut through Penn State's defense like a chain saw. He completed 18 of 30 passes for 280 yards and three touchdowns in a 26–10 victory. Coach Paterno stood silently as the final gun went off, no doubt wondering what he had missed when he first saw Jim Kelly play in high school.

Jim went on to shatter virtually every Hurricanes passing record, despite missing most of his senior year after an injury. When he had arrived at the University of Miami in 1978, the

Jim hands off to Chris Hobbs in the 1982 Peach Bowl. Jim was voted MVP of the game.

Jim Kelly blew defenses away during his two full seasons at Miami (1980-81)

YARDS

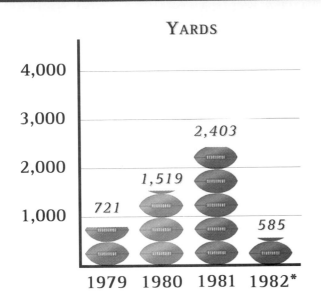

4,000

3,000

2,403

2,000

1,519

1,000

721

585

1979 1980 1981 1982*

TOUCHDOWNS

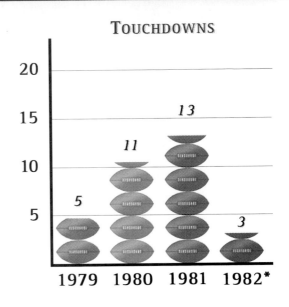

20

15

13

11

10

5

5

3

1979 1980 1981 1982*

*Missed most of senior season with injury

football team could not even fill its stadium. When Jim left, the Hurricanes were considered a national power.

Jim was the University of Miami's first great quarterback. After Jim graduated, two younger players—Bernie Kosar and Vinnie Testaverde—stepped into the Hurricanes' quarterback role and did well, too. All three went on to star in the NFL.

Bernie Kosar (left) and Vinnie Testaverde took over at quarterback after Jim left Miami.

Road to

University of Miami players Jim Kelly (left) and Mark Rush meet the press after signing contracts with the USFL Houston Gamblers.

Jim Kelly was selected by the Buffalo Bills with the 14th pick in the NFL draft. But he was also selected by the Chicago Blitz in the United States Football League (USFL) draft. Chicago did not think that Jim would sign with the new league and did not pursue him seriously. The Bills assumed that he would be content to sit on their bench while he learned from veteran passer Joe Ferguson. In a shocking turn of events, the Blitz traded their claim to Jim to the USFL Houston Gamblers. Jim signed a contract with the Gamblers to become their starting quarterback for the 1984 season.

Jim played for two seasons in the USFL, and during that time he piled up more passing yards and touchdowns than anyone in pro football history. In his rookie year, he threw for 5,219 yards and 44 touchdowns to win both the Rookie of the Year and

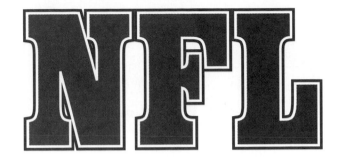

the NFL

Most Valuable Player awards. In his second season, Jim missed four games but still threw for 4,623 yards and 39 touchdowns.

Despite Jim's heroics, the Gamblers could not make enough money to continue in 1986. Many of the team's players, including Jim and two of his favorite receivers—Clarence Verdin and Ricky Sanders—went to the USFL New Jersey Generals. That made football fans sit up and take notice. Jim would join running back Herschel Walker, who had gained a pro record 2,411 yards the year before. The thought of Jim and Herschel in the same backfield was tremendously exciting. Would anyone be able to stop the Generals? Football fans never found out. The USFL could not draw enough fans to its games, and in 1986 the league went out of business.

Jim scrambles away from Memphis Showboats defensive end Reggie White.

The Story

After the USFL folded, Jim signed with the NFL Buffalo Bills and became the team's starting quarterback. Buffalo's offense was perfect for Jim. Instead of calling plays in the huddle, Jim and the rest of the Bills often walked up to the line, got into position, and took a good, long look at the defense. When Jim saw a weakness, he would bark out a series of signals to let his teammates know which play to run. This "no-huddle" offense rushed other teams into making mistakes, giving Jim and the Bills a big advantage.

Jim quickly established himself as one of the NFL's most consistent passers, and one of the toughest players around. In his very first game (against the New York Jets), he drew comparisons to his childhood hero, Joe Namath. He stood up to the Jets' top-notch pass rush and threw three touchdowns. Jim exhibited the kind of leadership and competitive fury the Bills had been missing for many years.

Continues

As the field general for the Buffalo Bills, Jim developed a reputation as a tough and intelligent quarterback.

In 1990, Jim survived a knee injury to lead Buffalo to its third straight division title. Jim completed more than 63 percent of his passes for 24 touchdowns and only 9 interceptions. His quarterback rating of 101.2 was not just the best in the league, it was one of the highest figures in history. In the playoffs, he won a 44–34 shootout with Dan Marino and the Miami Dolphins. The Bills obliterated the Raiders 51–3 to advance to Super Bowl XXV. There, Jim played magnificently against the

The no-huddle offense made it hard for teams to set up on defense against the high-scoring Bills.

New York Giants, completing 18 of 30 passes against the NFL's top defense. With two minutes left, Buffalo was behind by two points. Needing a field goal to win, Jim's offense got the ball on their own 10-yard line. Jim marched the team down the field, all the way to the Giants' 29. The Bills appeared to have the game won. But kicker Scott Norwood missed the field goal, sending the Bills home sad and disappointed.

Jim would return to the Super Bowl the next three years, but the Bills ran into hot teams each time and lost. Still, Kelly was only the third quarterback in history—Hall of Famers Sid Luckman and Otto Graham were the other two—to lead his team to four straight championship games.

In 1995, Jim surpassed 3,000 passing yards for the eighth season since coming to the NFL. If you count his two USFL seasons, Jim has had ten 3,000-yard campaigns, good for a second-place tie on the all-time list!

Jim's career statistics rank him with football's all-time great quarterbacks.

Timeline

1979: Becomes University of Miami starting quarterback

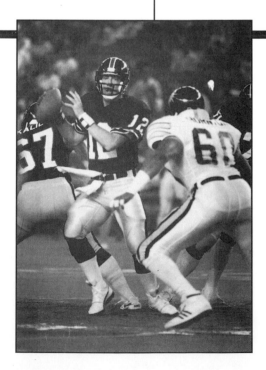

1983: Begins playing in the United States Football League

1977: Leads East Brady High School to the first of two undefeated seasons

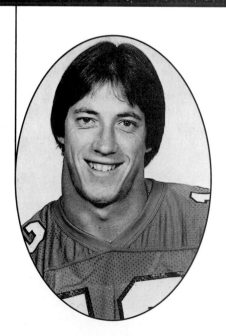

1986: Becomes the starting quarterback for the NFL Buffalo Bills

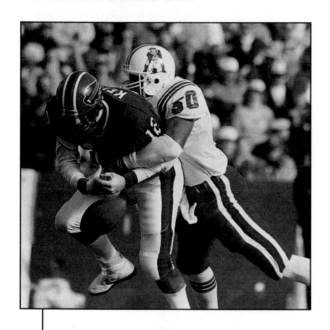

1994: Leads the Bills to their fourth straight Super Bowl appearance

1990: Records a quarterback rating of 101.2

1995: Tops 30,000 yards passing in NFL

Game

With the Houston Gamblers, Jim put up some of the biggest numbers in football history.

Although the USFL went out of business, Jim had fun while he played there. "I learned a lot in the USFL, and I had a good time."

Jim is willing to be tackled if it means giving his receivers an extra half-second to get open.

Action!

ou want to keep the defense guessing . . . that's a big part of football."

Jim is a master of the "hot read." When he spots a blitz, he sets up without dropping all the way back in the pocket and zips the ball to an open receiver.

You have to have a great quarterback to be successful, but you also have to have the wide receivers and the offensive line."

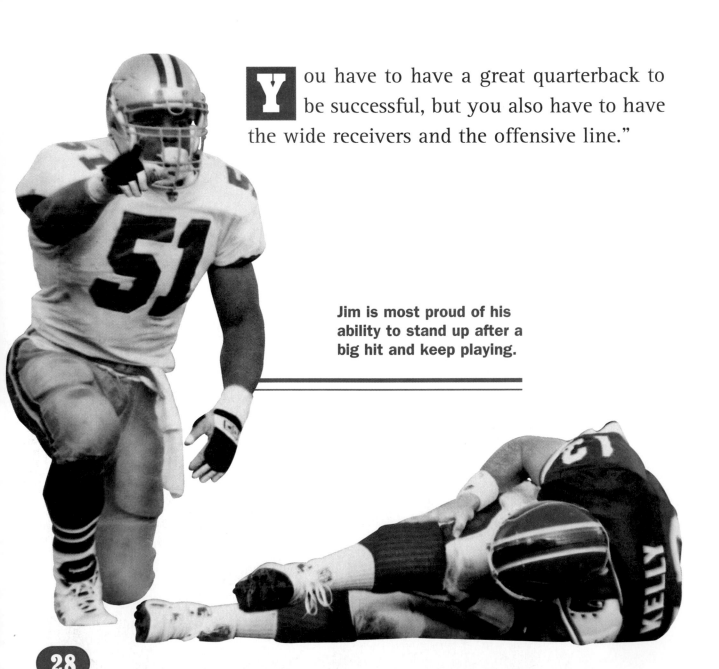

Jim is most proud of his ability to stand up after a big hit and keep playing.

Jim calls his own plays, but he also listens to his teammates in the huddle. He will revise his plans if a receiver says he can beat his man, or if a lineman feels he can open a hole.

"Who do I admire most in the game? More than anyone I admire my coach, Marv Levy."

Dealing

When Jim was 10, he reached the national semifinals of the Punt, Pass, and Kick contest. Showing great poise in front of a huge crowd at San Diego's Jack Murphy Stadium, he performed well in the first two parts of the competition. But in the kicking competition, disaster struck. A light rain had fallen the night before, and the grass was a little slick. As Jim planted

Jim (center) and Bernie Kosar (left) conduct a Punt, Pass, and Kick class. When Jim was 10, he was a national semi-finalist in the competition.

With It

his left foot and began to swing his right leg forward, he slipped and fell on his rear end. As he was going down, his right foot nicked the top of the ball and it trickled off the tee.

Jim was out of the competition. That day he learned that no matter how hard you try, things do not always work out perfectly. But he also learned that good things will follow the bad if you keep on trying. That lesson served him well after the Buffalo Bills lost four straight Super Bowls. Had Jim stopped trying after the first loss, he never would have made it to the next three. Having gone through so many ups and downs in his football career, Jim can now look back and laugh about his embarrassing moment in the Punt, Pass, and Kick contest. "I wasn't laughing then. I was crying!"

Jim learned early how to deal with disappointment. Here, Troy Aikman consoles him after a Super Bowl loss.

HOW DOES

Like any smart quarterback, Jim Kelly prefers to throw the ball to a receiver who is being covered by just one player. But what do you do when the receiver you want to throw to is double-covered? Jim knows that defensive players often look at a quarterback's eyes right after the ball is snapped in order to figure out where he is throwing. When they see Jim look at a receiver, they rush over to double-team that player. Jim creates single coverage by looking at a receiver he does *not* want to throw to. When the defense shifts toward that player, he quickly looks at his real target and delivers a perfect pass.

Jim prepares to throw left against the New England Patriots. Jim has already looked to his right to try to fool the defensive backs.

He Do It?

The Grind

Buffalo fans wave flags before the start of a Bills playoff game.
Jim is one of the Bills fans' favorite players.

Taking time to answer questions from the media is a daily routine for Jim.

Jim Kelly faces the same dilemma as other NFL stars. Because he only plays once a week, people think he has all the time in the world the other six days. Jim loves to hang out and talk football with fans. He tries to make as many appearances as possible in between meetings and practices, but eventually he runs out of time and has to turn people down.

"My mother always says that since you can't please everybody, don't try. Just go out there and be yourself. There's no way I can spend 20 minutes with everybody—there aren't enough hours in a day. I just try to treat people the same way I would like them to treat me."

Say What?

Here's what football people are saying about Jim Kelly:

"He's a good guy, and he's a tough guy."

—*Hank Bullough,*
  Jim's first coach with the Bills

"Jim is the best quarterback in football."

—*Donald Trump,*
  former owner of the USFL
  New Jersey Generals

"Give me the choice of any quarterback in this league and I'll take Jim Kelly."

—*Marv Levy,*
  Buffalo Bills head coach

"I don't think any player in the school's history has meant more to the University of Miami than Jim Kelly."

—*Howard Schnellenberger,*
Jim's college coach

"Kelly is a tough, courageous quarterback."

—*Paul Zimmerman, sportswriter*

"Kelly's teammates accept his blistering criticism, then hover around him after a game or practice."

—*Mickey Herskowitz, sportswriter*

"He's one tough player."

—*Mark Gastineau,*
former New York Jets
defensive linesman

"Jim's a great leader and a winner."

—*Andre Reed,*
Jim's favorite receiver

Career

Jim is one of only three quarterbacks in history to lead his team to four consecutive NFL championship games.

Highlights

Jim surpassed 30,000 career passing yards in a 1995 game against the Indianapolis Colts.

Steve Young and Jim once hooked up for 829 passing yards in a USFL contest. They topped that total with 852 yards in a 1992 Bills-49ers game.

Steve Young (left) and Jim (right) flank USFL commissioner Harry Usher (center). Both Jim and Steve are now All-Pros in the NFL.

Jim has played in the Pro Bowl four times. In 1991, he led the AFC to a thrilling comeback win and was named the game's Most Valuable Player. He completed 13 of 19 passes for 210 yards and a pair of touchdowns.

The Buffalo Bills sold 38,000 tickets in the six days after they signed Jim in 1986.

Jim led the University of Miami to the Peach Bowl in 1981. The Hurricanes defeated Virginia Tech, 20–10, and Jim was named the game's Most Valuable Player.

Jim has completed at least 60 percent of his passes in four different NFL seasons. In 1990, his 63.3% mark was the best in the league.

Jim led the Bills to a 51–3 defeat of the Raiders in the 1990 AFC Championship game. The margin of victory was the largest in history for a conference title game.

Reaching

For more than a hundred years, disadvantaged and disabled children from western New York state spent a couple of weekends each summer at Cradle Beach Camp on the shore of Lake Erie. Over the years, thousands of kids were able to go swimming and camping there. They also learned to get along with children different than themselves in a building that has been called the "Big House." Sadly, the Big House fell into disrepair, and Cradle Beach did not have the money to fix it up. When Jim Kelly got to Buffalo, he heard about this special place and wanted to be a part of it. In 1993, his Kelly for Kids Foundation pledged $500,000 to help rebuild the Big House. With Jim's help, Cradle Beach got a great start on its second century! Jim also sponsors Kelly's Community Grant Program, which awards $2,500 each week during the football season to youth-oriented charities in the Buffalo area. Jim announces the recipients each week on his television show, "Bills Sneak Preview with Jim Kelly."

Out

Jim visits with the victim
of a spinal-cord injury

Jim joins fellow
quarterbacks Brett Favre,
Dan Marino, and Drew
Bledsoe (left to right)
at a benefit for the
Tomorrow's Children Fund.

Numbers

Name: James Edward Kelly

Born: February 14, 1960

Height: 6' 3"

Weight: 230 pounds

Uniform Number: 12

College: University of Miami

Jim wore number 11 in high school, but he switched to 12 in college because both of his favorite players, Joe Namath and Terry Bradshaw, wore the number.

Season	Team	Attempts	Completions	Pct.	Yards	TDs	QB Rating
1984	Houston Gamblers	587*	370*	63.0	5,219*	44*	98.2
1985	Houston Gamblers	567*	360*	63.5	4,623*	39*	97.9
USFL Total**		1,154	730	63.3	9,842	83	98.1

Season	Team	Attempts	Completions	Pct.	Yards	TDs	QB Rating
1986	Buffalo Bills	480	285	59.4	3,593	22	83.3
1987	Buffalo Bills	419	250	59.7	2,798	19	83.8
1988	Buffalo Bills	452	269	59.5	3,380	15	78.2
1989	Buffalo Bills	391	228	58.3	3,130	25	86.2
1990	Buffalo Bills	346	219	63.3*	2,829	24	101.2*
1991	Buffalo Bills	474	304	64.1	3,844	33*	97.6
1992	Buffalo Bills	462	269	58.2	3,457	23	81.2
1993	Buffalo Bills	470	288	61.3	3,382	18	79.9
1994	Buffalo Bills	448	285	63.6	3,114	22	84.6
1995	Buffalo Bills	458	255	55.7	3,130	22	81.1
NFL Total		4,400	2,652	60.3	32,657	223	85.4

* Led League

** USFL stats are not recognized by the NFL

What If...

I have had three operations to repair football injuries in my life. Each time, there was a possibility that I might never play again. And each time—beginning in college—I thought about what I would do if I had to give up the game. That's a big reason why I studied business management in school. Like a lot of my friends, I had no idea what kind of job I might want to do. But I figured that knowing how a business runs would help me in any career. As for what I plan to do after my playing days, I think it would be nice to be a coach. I wouldn't want to work at the high level of the NFL or college. I'd prefer to work with kids, perhaps as a youth-league or high-school coach."

Glossary

DILEMMA a situation involving difficult choices

ELIGIBLE possessing the needed abilities to perform a task

EXCLUSIVE open or available to only a certain person or group

FOLDED collapsed; came to an end; no longer in operation

COMPARISON an examination of likenesses and differences

CONSECUTIVE several events that follow one after another

CRITICISM the act of saying what is good or bad about something; disapproval

OBLITERATE to destroy all traces of; to make disappear

RECRUITED asked to join a team or organization

SCHOLARSHIP money given to a student to help pay for schooling

VETERAN one who has had a lot of experience

INCLINED (ATHLETICALLY) having a natural talent for; drawn toward a certain activity

LACKED needed a missing ingredient

LUCRATIVE well paying; profitable

Index

About The Author

Mark Stewart grew up in New York City in the 1960s and 1970s—when the Mets, Jets, and Knicks all had championship teams. As a child, Mark read everything about sports he could lay his hands on. Today, he is one of the busiest sportswriters around. Since 1990, he has written close to 500 sports stories for kids, including profiles on more than 200 athletes, past and present. A graduate of Duke University, Mark served as senior editor of *Racquet*, a national tennis magazine, and was managing editor of *Super News*, a sporting goods industry newspaper. He is the author of every Grolier All-Pro Biography.